Duelling Poets

Also by Michelle Gordon:

Fiction:
Earth Angel Series:
The Earth Angel Training Academy
The Earth Angel Awakening
The Other Side
The Twin Flame Reunion
The Twin Flame Retreat
The Twin Flame Resurrection
The Twin Flame Reality
The Twin Flame Rebellion
The Twin Flame Reignition
The Twin Flame Resolution

Visionary Collection
Heaven dot com
The Doorway to PAM
The Elphite
I'm Here

The Magical Doorway Series
The Magical Faerie Door

Non-fiction:
Where's My F**king Unicorn?

Also by Victor Keegan:

Remember to Forget
Crossing the Why
Big Bang
Alchemy of Age
London My London

Duelling Poets

Michelle Gordon
&
Victor Keegan

Turquoise
Quill
Press

All rights reserved; no part of this book may be reproduced, stored in a retrieval system, or transmitted, in any form or by any means, without the prior permission in writing from the publisher, nor be otherwise circulated in any form of binding or cover other than that in which it is published and without a similar condition including this condition being imposed on the subsequent purchaser.

First published in Great Britain in 2020 by Turquoise Quill Press
An Imprint of Not From This Planet

NotFromThisPlanet.co.uk

Copyright © 2020 Michelle Gordon & Victor Keegan
Cover Image by Art Lasovsky (unsplash)
Cover Design by The Amethyst Angel

ISBN: 978-1-912257-60-7

The moral rights of the authors have been asserted.

All characters and events in this publication, other than those clearly in the public domain are fictitious, and any resemblance to real persons, living or dead, is purely coincidental.

First Edition

Acknowledgements

This book has take a long time to get to publication, so I'd like to thank everyone who has been waiting for it for their patience!

And thank you Victor, for duelling with me!
~ *Michelle*

A big thank you to Michelle, whose idea this was all those years ago, and without whom it would never have made the journey from emails to print. Enjoy.
~ *Victor*

In 2012, two poets challenged one another to a duel.
A poem a day for 30 days.
Each day, they would write a poem with the same title.

Now, it's up to you to decide who wins.

Simply tick the boxes of your favourite poems, then at the end of the book, you can see who wrote which one, and add up the score for each poet.

Then share your winner on Twitter!

1a. Miracles

Miracle Muse is like you and me
Except everywhere around
She can plainly see
That miracles abound
Which happen without even making a sound
What do you make of that?

The world she sees is what we observe
Who are low on the psychic learning curve
But where we see a coincidence plain
She sees Providence at work again
What do you make of that?

1b. Miracles

They happen every day.
Most slip by,
Unnoticed by most.
Their every-day nature,
Camouflages their existence.

But they are there.
They do not require our attention,
Our gratitude
Or our praise.
They happen every day,
Regardless.

But if you were to notice them,
Appreciate them
And give thanks for them,
You may find that they increase.
In number and
In intensity.

Until one day you realise
That you are completely surrounded
By miracles.

2a. Talent

I wish I had the kind of talent
That could silence a room
That could inspire millions
That could change the world.

I wish I had the kind of talent
That I could make a living from
That I could feel proud of
That would be admired by others.

I wish I had talent.

2b. Talent

Had I the talent so to do
Many Mandalas would I paint for you
Your unconscious world to journey to
From which returning travellers are few

But I having no talent so to paint
Offer these verses in restraint
You can read into them what you will
Your own Mandala thus to fill

3a. Mandala

I found myself
In a strange land
meditating before a Mandala
one of those circular
patterned paintings
Hindhu I think
that are said to induce trances
or penetrate the unconscious
But it was a long time ago
and I am now wondering whether
it was all a dream
like much of my past
Or whether it makes any difference

3b. Mandala

A blank canvas
A dinner plate
Some pencil lines
Metallic paints
A pattern emerges
Geometric yet off-centre
But there is a reason for this.

I don't paint for the fun of it
I don't paint because I'm good at it
I don't paint for other people
I paint with intent

In each brushstroke
I am infusing the qualities
Of the one I seek
The one who completes me
The one who makes sense
Of these patterns.

My mandala is my soulmate
In colours and patterns
Created on a blank canvas
With a dinner plate.

4a. Church

In their mission to unify us,
They divided us.

In their mission to create peace,
They created wars.

In their efforts to spread the word of God,
They distorted his very soul.

In their efforts to find saints,
They made us all sinners.

In their preaching of the truth,
They lost sight of it completely.

In their avid search for followers,
They created protesters.

In their acceptance of repentance,
They created indifference.

Go to church on Sunday?
No thanks.

4b. Church

I go to a church inside my head
No Heaven, no Hell, just me instead
There's a dome and columns too
Stained glass and my personal pew
Designed by Hawksmoor to fire my mind
Into imaginings of an ethereal kind
Where problems cease
There I find peace
In the Mandala of Now
Where no one else can go

5a. Modesty

Modesty left town in the sixties
And hasn't come back
Driven out by shortening skirts
Cleavage
And four letter words

Gone, but not forgotten
I sometimes dream about you
And drool over
An erotic innocence
That is no longer.
One day you'll come back,
I'll hazard a bet
And be welcomed in my home
It's just that, well, please God,
Not yet

5b. Modesty

Modesty is the way of this nation.
To toot one's own horn
Is one of the highest of wrongs
One can commit.
To be proud of ones achievements
Is vulgar.
To be happy with one's life
Is arrogant.
To shoot for the stars
Is going above one's station
To want more from one's life
Is greedy.
To want to succeed
Is selfish.

But I believe that
Modesty is the plague
Of our great nation.
That we should be happy,
Confident,
And proud.
Of who we are,
And what we achieve.

Now if you'll excuse me,
I need to go toot my horn.

6a. Malvern Hills

Go, meander, absorb
The Malverns
Step out of time
Retreat to bygone days
For everything is the same.
If Piers Plowman woke up now
From his big sleep
Toiling the fields
Those years ago
He might carrry on
Not knowing
The world has changed
That's why I
Too, now, go, there
To feel the same.

6b. Malvern Hills

It may be a popular destination,
For holidays and retirement.
It may look beautiful in the sun,
And mysterious in the misty grey.
It may be the subject of art
And literature world-wide.

But for me,
This place is filled
With nothing but memories,
Of lost time,
Feelings of
Sadness,
And echoes of the longing
For something more.

So every time,
I journey back here
I can't help wishing,
I were somewhere else.

7a. Socks

"Pull your socks up"
Said my teacher in primary school
When I played the fool
And made her wince
And have done so ever since.

You can of course pull your socks up
Without actually pulling your socks up
It's just a figure of speech upended.

But figures of speech can have holes in them too
Which ought to be mended
But not this one.
You can always do a little better
If you pull your socks up.

7b. Socks

The happiest time
Of my life was spent with you
In your arms. Content.

We dreamed together
Slept, laughed and cried together
We fit together.

The end came too soon
The house is now bare. Empty
Of my scent, and me.

The only sign that
I was here, are two lonely
Old, dirty odd socks.

8a. Memory

I want to be
The one by your side.
I want to be
The one in whom you confide.

I want to be
The first one you call.
I want to be
The one who catches you when you fall.

I want to be
The one holding your hand.
I want to be
The one you build castles with in the sand.

I want to be
The one you kiss goodnight.
I want to be
The one you hold so tight.

I want to be
Your everything, forever.

I don't want to be
Just a memory.

8b. Memory

We grow our own memories, don't we?
It's like weeding the garden,
Killing off nettles that might sting.
That way I convinced myself to say:
"We really had quite a good holiday
The row before last didn't happen
I remembered your birthday
And I did return the book from that library then.
And I left you, not you, me."
I feel better already, see.

Amnesia erases a bad memory
It's our own PR system, you might say
So we can all look forward to a happier day.
Memory doesn't play tricks with us
We play tricks with it.
It's part of our survival kit.

9a. Birdsong

No one lives without birdsong
though they may be unaware
it is there. Even when it isn't
a constant presence, you'll find
a never ending reverberation
in the echo chamber of the mind;
ever fainter but ever there
without anger, without malice,
a spring of joy, constant solace,
an ambient fraternity,
In lingering eternity.
Birdsong, birdsong
You are there, all along.

9b. Birdsong

At dawn it begins,
The rising sun their cue.
It begins softly, as they awake,
One by one, from slumber
Upon their branches.
As the sky lightens
The tempo increases,
More voices join in.
The first of the sun's rays
Hit the trees
And the harmony rises
To a dramatic crescendo.

Throughout the day
Nature's magnificent,
Invisible orchestra
Continues to play.
There are solos, harmonies
And lone, soulful notes.
Then dusk comes,
The conducting sun
Goes to sleep,
And the final notes
Fade into the darkness.

10a. Journey

We are all on a journey
Even when sitting still
(Think world revolving on its axis
But also shooting around the sun,
Itself part of a galloping galaxy).

My journey is simpler:
From me to you
A tiny distance in time
But too great a leap for mankind
It seems. Truth is, the saddest fact
It takes two to make a friendship intact
And the shortest trip for me
Is the longest journey
For you. Closeness
Keeps us apart.

10b. Journey

I have experienced far more
Perilous journeys
Than this one.
In my previous existences
I have experienced war,
Starvation,
Damnation,
And pain.
But no amount of pain
Ever experienced before,
Will come close to the torture
Of having experienced your touch,
only to lose you,
What feels like a second
Later.
Must I continue this journey alone?
If so, I hope it goes quickly,
And that perhaps in the next world,
We find one another once more.
For my journey is pointless,
Endless
And hopeless.
Without you.

11a. Whisper

Hey, she whispered
Do you think you could change the topic?
To what? he replied,
What life is like on Mars?
No, she retorted.
Though I do wonder what
The milky way looks like,
Close up.
He snickered. How about
Dreams? I dreamt last night
I got run over by a
Double decker.
That's nothing,
She declared,
I dreamt I had a picnic
In a beautiful garden of roses.
What's so unusual about that?
He asked. You're such a flake.
She twirled away from him in disgust.
I've had enough of you, Mr Fudge,
I'm calling a time out.

11b. Whisper

They stalk me everywhere,
these whisperings
following me like a sound shadow.
That isn't there when I turn
Will no one tell me to my face
In case I learn a secret
shared by all but me.
They stop when I enter the village shop
and start again as I leave.
I am woken up in the night
by ghostly whisperings
which fade away, then more
like waves on the shore
Getting nearer each time
rising from cold to warm
building into a storm
assailing my head
as I hide in my bed.
You say, trying to be kind,
That it's all in the mind
That I am not going insane
But that just adds
To the whispering campaign

12a. Too Many Questions

Forgo, I say, stop, desist
Yet still you carry on, persist
Questions, questions, always asking
Testing me for multi-tasking
Too many things you ask of me
I have no answers You can see
And when you deem my replies frugal
You smile at me and go to Google
Search engines for sure are all the rage
But they do not solve the issues of the age
Of God, of Love, of co-existence
Of humility and dogged persistence
They give us no informed instruction
How to avoid assured destruction
Life has too many questions left
But more than that I am bereft
I have no answers to pursue
Is that not good enough for you?

12b. Too Many Questions

The pendulum swings
Waiting to decide my fate.
What to ask first?
Should I ask about money?
About my relationship?
My career?
My future?
Maybe I should ask what to do next,
What I should focus on.
Or perhaps where I should live,
Or travel to.
The pendulum swings on,
And I ask my questions in quick succession.
Within a matter of minutes,
I have my answers.
I can see my future clearly.

And now I wish I hadn't asked.

13a. SynchroniCity

From such a distance it seems a pity
You've never heard of Synchroni City
For what you've missed is a galactic game
For it is London Town in all but name
Every inhabitant, you need not fear
Is exactly replicated here
And so it is throughout the earth
Everyone's had a twin since birth
And shadowed in another universe
Yes, the entire human race
Is replicated in another place
All designed by a universal force
But you can't get in touch of course
Because communicating would shatter
Your parallel identity and that would matter
For you'd cease to be parallel but linked
So, in effect, this means no longer synched
Best not to dwell on synchronicity
Just wallow in the serendipity.

13b. Synchronicity

You may think,
That it was chance
That brought us together.
Pure, random coincidence.
That our meeting meant nothing,
That it bears no significance
To our lives,
Or to the world.
But I know the truth.
I know that our meeting was designed.
That is was set up
By the same powers
That control the universe.
We are merely the puppets of the gods,
Playing out their desires
In our words and actions.
They intended for us to meet.
I wonder if we will ever find out
Why.

14a. Embarking

When we embark on this epic journey,
That is life
We know all that we have been
All that we will be
All what we will experience
All that will go well,
All that will go wrong.
We are one,
We are connected to all
Through the threads
That make up the universe.
And with that first
Shuddering,
Gasping breath
We forget it all.
We forget who we are,
Who we were
And who we will be.
Some of us will remember,
But for most, it will remain forgotten
Until we take out last breath.
And embark on our next adventure.

14b. Embarking

Go on a journey if it pleases you
It is a free country, yours to pursue
Or you could leave a classier mark
You could Embark
That adds value immediately
Embarkation has a sense of mission, longevity
The Pilgrim Fathers did not GO to America
steerage
They EMBARKED on a voyage
As did Drake and Magellan
Would it therefore be too phoney
If I asked you to embark on a journey
With me alone
Destiny unknown
Just say Nay or Aye
Please don't embark on a long reply.

15a. Mugs

Buying mugs used to be such an easy decision
Just painted white with no precision
Now they come in all shapes and sizes
Wondrous colours, full of surprises
What a variety, what a lotta
From Mickey Mouse to Harry Potter

But me
What would I like to see?
I've got no time for that fancy lot
I want a picture of myself,
My own, my very own, mugshot.

15b. Mugs

When you have a favourite one,
It is almost impossible
To drink from any other vessel.
You will hunt it down,
Wash it out,
And scream at anyone who may have dared
To use it.
Battered, chipped,
Stained, cracked,
Pattern faded, handle missing,
It doesn't matter what state
It is in,
Your favourite mug
Will never be thrown away,
Because tea will never taste right
Without it.

16a. May

In May,
All will become clear.
The clouds will part,
The doubts will depart,
And certainty shall be your friend once more.
But as the days stroll by
I begin to doubt these wise words
As the clouds stay firmly in place.
I do my best to stay in the present
To not stray into the murky waters
Of the past,
Or the hazy vagueness
Of the future.
But I long to know,
What will happen,
When and how.
I guess I will just have to believe
That when May comes to an end
The clouds will clear
And I will know.

16b. May

April may be the cruellest month
Who am I to say
But May is in a class of its own
However the weathermen drone
It can't make up its mind
Whether it is premature summer,
A seasonal bummer
An incipient Spring having a fling
Or a lingering memory of Winter's sting.
It is the only month that's aptly named
It may be fine, it may have rained
It may have drought
It may have nowt
On May Day there may be revolution
But more likely a softer solution
But whatever it is
We won't know it in advance
Because May, like a lover
Keeps its advances under cover
I don't wish to be unkind
I just wish they both would make up their mind.

17a. Magic

We were destined to meet, or so you claim.
I say just chance. Maybe it's all the same
Just serendipity in all but name
You happened to be there and I just came
At the same time as you, a happy chance
That's a logical view, no need to advance
Old wives' tales and medieval fixes
Spiritual theories and metaphysics.
But there's one little thing I have to concede
Something has happened that has filled a need
Conjuring these poems out of nothing
Has brought a little magic to my life, you see
But I don't know whether I am destined to be
A magician with clout
Or a manipulated puppet without
I wonder if I will ever find out.

17b. Magic

They say that it is dead.
They say that it doesn't exist.
They say it has fizzled out.
They say it is a myth.
They say it is nothing but imagination.
They say that to believe in it,
Is madness.

But if they would just stop,
For a moment,
And observe the world around them,
Then they would see
That it is
Magic
That we are made of.
Magic
That the fabric of the Universe
Is woven from.
Magic
That brought us together.
Magic
That connects us,
Even when we are apart.
And it will be
Magic
That will join us together
Forever.

18a. If

If only I had
The time to write this poem
And do it justice

But the late hour
And the promise of pleasure
Have stolen my words

I promise to do
Better tomorrow, only
If

18b. If

He was brought up a Catholic,
Roman persuasion
Which he followed religiously
On every occasion
How could it be anything other
Without huge domestic bother.
Of course, if he'd been reared Hindhu
The same would have been true
If he'd been born in a Muslim country
A devote Islamist he would now be
If he'd been placed in a school of extremism
A suicide bomber would have been his realism
Believing he was doing God's word
No doubts would ever have occured
For doubts don't occur if Truth's on your side
And if they did, you'd still go along for the ride
Even if it turned out to be, well
A one-way ticket to hell
But this word presumes that hell exists
When it's only folk law that somehow persists.
The moral of this is plain to see
What you believe is not related to Truth
But something more mundane: geography
Such beliefs can't be all right
But they could be all wrong
And with that I will end my song
Knowing it won't do any good- no one will act
For the truth is that fiction is stronger than fact.

19a. Groove

You may think it's groovy to go to a movie
But the new generation doesn't see
It that way. They think you're caught in a groove
Like a vinyl record which they don't approve
You need Style not a stylus if you want to be cool
Or else be dismissed as a retro fool
Who can't move from the grooves on which he turns
Like stuck needles on a Sixties LP he never learns
So drop the word groovy, grab today's tool
And at least be ungroovy if you can't be cool.

19b. Groove

The worn, weathered, faded
Wooden boards
Creak gently beneath my feet.
My bare soles feel every groove,
And grain.
Though it may appear to some
As if I am walking the plank,
In fact, I am walking,
Slowly,
Certainly,
And happily
Towards my destiny.
As the waves gently break
My gaze never wavers
From the only one that matters.
You.

20a. The Doward

Observe the Wye, a serpent path it winds
Around the hill dubbed Doward with its trees
Among the rocks and garlic groves it finds
A perfumed ride through cliff tops to the seas

It was not all bliss among these gorges
Despite the heights of Wordsworth's magic tour
They once made iron here in smokey forges
That made the hill a bleak industrial sore

The industrial revolution could
Have happened here instead of further north
They had the river, water, iron, and wood
The trouble was no money coming forth

Yet poets praised its beauty to the skies
We have to sort the licence from the lies

20b. The Doward

I have never felt more safe,
Loved, cherished
And happy,
Than I have in these woods.
Hidden from the world,
In a bubble of contentment.

But I have also never felt
So afraid,
So broken, and so lost,
As I have in these woods.
Every time I leave
And say goodbye,
Another part of me dies.

I hope that one day
These woods will be
My sanctuary of peace
And the memories of
Anything else
Will have faded away.

21a. The Shower

You were a shower
Of fresh rain
Coming unexpectedly
Over the hills
Dropping from the skies
Cooling, refreshing
Invigorating me
Before evaporating
Into the air you had sprung from
Where you are now I do not know
I wish I had asked your name
But you are still here
In memory
Does the same rain
Ever come to the same place.
Again.

21b. The Shower

Heart shaped bubbles
On the shower-room wall
Send my imagination
Into a freefall

If everything has meaning,
Then the universe must surely
Be trying to send me a message
But what could it be?

They slide slowly down
Losing and regaining their shape
As they go
What does it mean?

Then your arms encircle me
And my fascination ends.
It no longer seems important
To decipher the message
From the heart shaped bubbles
On the shower-room wall.

22a. The Painting

If only I were an artist,
And I could paint my love
For you.
I'd use bright hues,
Purples, pinks, reds and blues.
With every brushstroke
I'd imagine you by my side,
With every line and curve
I'd see your hand in mine.
A masterpiece it would be,
My love for you, and yours for me,
A lasting monument
For everyone to see.

But I am no artist,
Only my words do I have to give
And I fear they do not
Do our love justice,
And for that I hope you can forgive
Me.

22b. The Painting

If I could paint you as I choose
What wondrous colours would I use
Shall I go get oils so to do
A picture that shows all of you
Some parts cubist it could be
To catch your inner self. I'd see
Shades of you as impressionist
Merging your features in a mist
Mostly though I'd I see you from afar
For that's the way you really are.

Hell, what's the point of a painter's view
If I can have the actual you
Not as a picture on the wall
But changing every time I call
A living, giving, caring prospect
Steeped in love from every aspect
No need to share with anyone else
When I can have you for myself
Beaming on me all through the day
Without a canvas getting in the way.

23a. The Key

Had I the key to happiness
Many duplicates would I make
And hand them out along the street
To every passer-by I meet
But I have no such keys.
Happiness can't be turned on
With a key in the door or switch on the wall
Suddenly to give contentment to all.
But you can do something and play your part.
Put a smile on your face when you start your day
And keep it with you through work and play
You'll find it gets passed on to others
Who can't help but smile back or beam
And who'll pass it on like a virus or meme.
It won't change the world in whole or in part
But, for heaven's sake, at least it's a start.

23b. The Key

Battered and worn,
Dented and out of shape
Tired of trying to find
The perfect fit.

Having travelled for miles
And many, many years
I longed to find
The place I belonged.

Unless you are the master
And can open up the masses
There is only one
You will ever unlock.

I am no master,
I am a mere original
And I will not stop
Until I find the one.

The one who completes me
The one who makes my life
Worthwhile
And purposeful.

One day, I know
I will look upon them
And I will fit
The hole in their heart.

24a. Eating Out

You may think
That it's the short skirts,
Red lips
And subtle perfume
That makes her irresistible
To him.
Or maybe that it's the seductive
Body language,
The suggestive smile
Or the soft, sweet tones
Of her honey voice,
That has him eating
Out of the palm of her hand.
But I know better.
Many men have fallen
Into her trap,
Only to discover
That her angelic appearance
Is merely an illusion.
But by then it is too late.
She will have already stolen their soul
For her demonic collection
Kept beneath us
In the raging fires.

24b. Eating out

Eating out, it's plain to see
Is nothing like it used to be
Once it was just fish and chips
But now you've got the whole world's fare
From Kentucky fried to Heston rare
And thanks to Delia and Goddess Lawson
Cooking at home has become so awesome
You hardly need to go out as a foursome
The only value added is grabbed by mine host
Through a 300 per cent profit on most
Of the wines - plus Vat and service as well
Which can turn the meal into gastronomic hell.
So the moral of this is plain to see
Stay at home to cook and be
Celebrity chef to your spouse
Haute cuisine without leaving the house

25a. The Moon

Walking beneath
The moonlight
The stars are witness
To this unusual event.

Dressed to impress
A united front they represent
Raising awareness
Of the thief

The thief that has robbed them
Of mothers,
Grandmothers
And daughters.

As they march forwards
Under the watchful stars
Their love and kindness
Will make all the difference

Between those affected
Stumbling in the dark,
And having their path lit up
By the rays of the moon.

25b. The Moon

Great solar-powered torch
In the sky
How you ever got there, one
wonders why.
Creation's bastard child
Lifeless, inert
A giant fossil you are
Doing no useful work
Except as a mammoth reflector
Luring lovers into moonlit coves
Revellers into inns
So many ill met by moonlight
Committing sins
But all the time reminding us
The sun's still there.
For if the Moon goes out
The world will be bare
So thank you moon just
For being there.

26a. Tomorrow

Tomorrow never comes
At least literally.
There is never a moment when
You can say: "This is tomorrow"
It always moves ahead of you
An unreachable bourne
Like true love
Or the ever distancing
horizon line
True love, like tomorrow
Is for dreamers
So dream on,
You'll love it
Truly.

26b. Tomorrow

Oh no, not again
Surely it must be over
By now??
It feels like I've written
A hundred anthologies,
Is it really only
Day 26?
I've got editing to do,
Washing up in the sink
And sleep to catch up on.
I know I keep asking
For extensions
But perhaps you
Will permit me
One more -
Please, please
Could I write this poem
Tomorrow?

27a. The Bike

I thought it would be a bicycle
Something I could show my friends
But it turned out to be a bike
No flash handlebars, no lightness
It even had mudguards,
And weighed a ton
Oh dear
I know they intended well
No way can I go cycling in that thing
I might be seen
It will have to stay where it belongs
In the bike shed,
The museum of dead transportation
While I cycle on in my dreams.

27b. The Bike

After my bike
Died of rust
When I was five years old,
It was thrown in a skip.
My BMXing days were over.
Years passed,
Fear grew,
And I thought
I would never ride a bike
Again.
But that was until
I fell in love.
Love overcame my fear,
And now I ride
My gleaming silver bike
Every day,
Rain or shine.
So fear less,
Love more
And get on your bike!

28a. The Train

Don't see it as a train,
Ever again,
A hunk of metal,
Probably imported,
Carrying crusty commuters
To jobs they hate,
A stretched cube
Propelled along parallel lines
By fuel from a power station
Polluting the nation.

Think instead of a travelling office,
A rambling restaurant,
A brief encounter in a carriage
Leading to a hasty marriage
A poet's inspiration
A train of thought
For the lonely
With no destination
Excepting only
The terminus of
Imagination.

28b. The Train

No matter what I do
You manage to seek me out
No matter how much distance
I put between us
You always find me.
I tried my best,
This time
To change my future
To go forwards
On my own
Without you.
But once again
I have failed
Because here I am
On the train
And there you are
Sitting opposite me.

29a. Destiny

It may appear
That we each have
A destiny.
A path we should follow
A place we should end up
And certain things we should achieve
Along the way.
But no matter what
Our destinies decree
Our free will
Will always
Reign supreme.
It may be my destiny
To shine.
But if I choose to hide
In the darkness,
No angel of destiny
Can stop me.

29b. Destiny

Destiny is some place you are heading for
Unless it is heading for you.
So, I am asked to write a poem about destiny
Which makes me
Destined to write it.
But not predestined
Right?
I could stop writing this, you know
Just like that.
Except . . .
Shit, it's too late,
It's done.
Destiny, don't mess with me
Or there'll be consequences.
You'll see.

30a. Jubilee

As I was standing
In a 12 deep crowd
Jubilantly
Clustered by Lambeth Bridge
I saw her pass by
Momentarily
For a fraction of a second
Framed between someone's arm
And someone else's periscope
As her barge flowed under the bridge.
So, I have seen her
Yes, in the flesh
For the first time
For a minute fraction of
Her 60 year reign,
She, who still breathes longevity
In the age of Twitter.

30b. Jubilee

For some
It is a genuine
Celebration.
For others,
It's just an excuse
For a party.
For me,
It is just another Sunday.
But as long as it is
Promoting unity
And not segregation.
Then it will be a day
Worth remembering.

Time to Score!

Poem

1A - Victor
1B - Michelle

2A - Michelle
2B - Victor

3A - Victor
3B - Michelle

4A - Michelle
4B - Victor

5A - Victor
5B - Michelle

6A - Victor
6B - Michelle

7A - Victor
7B - Michelle

8A - Michelle
8B - Victor

9A - Victor
9B - Michelle

10A - Victor
10B - Michelle

11A - Michelle
11B - Victor

12A - Victor
12B - Michelle

13A - Victor
13B - Michelle

14A - Michelle
14B - Victor

15A - Victor
15B - Michelle

16A - Michelle
16B - Victor

17A - Victor
17B - Michelle

18A - Michelle
18B - Victor

19A - Victor
19B - Michelle

20A - Victor
20B - Michelle

21A - Victor
21B - Michelle

22A - Michelle
22B - Victor

23A - Victor
23B - Michelle

24A - Michelle
24B - Victor

25A - Michelle
25B - Victor

26A - Victor
26B - Michelle

27A - Victor
27B - Michelle

28A - Victor
28B - Michelle

29A - Michelle
29B - Victor

30A - Victor
30B - Michelle

Final Points

Michelle -

Victor -

And the winner is....

When you have a winner, please sure your result on Twitter using the hashtags -

#MichelleWinsTheDuel

#VictorWinsTheDuel

with the general hashtag #duellingpoets

Please tag Victor - @vickeegan
Michelle - @themiraclemuse
and Not From This Planet - @NFTPBooks

Thank you!

About Victor

Victor's life is split between Herefordshire where he relaxes, and London where he lives and does his walks (including one from Trafalgar Square to Margate without crossing a single road).

After 40 years of editing and writing for *The Guardian*, he now writes a weekly *Lost London* column for **OnLondon.co.uk**, as well as his own blogs, **LondonMyLondon.co.uk** and **VictorKeegan.wordpress.com** (about the UK wine revolution).

Poems, Victor says, are the most flexible and creative of all literary communication as they can be short or long, they can rhyme or not, and scan or not. No subject is off-limits.

You can follow Victor on Twitter - **@vickeegan**

To purchase Victor's other books on Amazon visit:
viewauthor.at/victorkeegan

About Michelle

Michelle lives in the UK, when she's not flitting in and out of other realms. She believes in Faeries and Unicorns and thinks the world needs more magic and fun in it. She writes because she would go crazy if she didn't. She has written several novels and a unicorn-themed self help book, and is always in the process of writing more!

Please feel free to write a review of this book. Michelle loves to get direct feedback, so if you would like to contact her, please visit her website or keep up to date by following her blog – **TwinFlameBlog.com.** You can also follow her on Twitter - **@themiraclemuse,** Instagram - **@michellegordonauthor** or like her page on Facebook.

To sign up to her mailing list, visit:
michellegordon.co.uk

To buy her other books, visit:
viewauthor.at/michellegordon

Books By Victor Keegan
Crossing The Why

Crossing the Why is Victor Keegan's first book of poems. It covers subjects from the meaning of life to travels in Provence. This is the first poem in *Crossing the Why* which was launched in 2001 in conjunction with a new website which used a remote computer to replicate a two line poem at the front of the book. After running 24/7 for nearly twenty years it has only got 13 characters right and that was 15 years ago! It is still trying at shakespearesmonkey.co.uk

Crossing the Why

Why am I here?
wondered a little girl
looking up from
her face in
the pool
at the staring stars.
You are here,
came the answer,
because of two
preposterous propositions.
One is that all of this,
the sun, the earth,
sudden mirth
the shooting stars
planets like Mars
the ones and noughts
of our secret thoughts
all came from an exploding speck
fifteen billion years ago
Before which there was

Nothing
And I don't mean space
I mean absolute
Nothing
the absence of everything.

Or - that God,
the first mover's First Mover,
created everything,
the moon, the flowers
the passing hours
our own free will
the urge to kill
from the same nothing.

And which of these propositions
should I choose
asked the girl,
throwing her last pebble
into the pool?
That's easy,
said the voice, with a clue.
The less preposterous of the two.

Big Bang

Big Bang, Victor Keegan's second poetry book, was first published in the virtual word Second Life at a gathering attended by avatars from around the world who engaged in an animated conversation about digital literature. The poems include seven about Truth, four about the artist Damien Hirst and many others ranging from the beginning of time to a sonnet on the River Wye.

Raynes Park

Everyone has a Raynes Park
in the suburbs of their minds,
somewhere to go as life gets hard,
a bottomless pool of childhood bliss,
where all was good that could be good,
apple trees, bikes, recreation grounds,
scrumping, laughing and paper rounds
the sound of birds that sang unseen
and green the most imagined sheen
on drip-dry afternoons that had no end
and all that was bad is lost in time
and the need to survive.
Everyone needs a Raynes Park
though they may not call it that
though ours was a special one
It's still there when we need it most
and have nowhere else to go.

Remember to Forget

Victor Keegan's third book of poems, *Remember to Forget,* is a journey from early childhood memories to encounters in virtual worlds taking in such diverse subjects as the end of the red telephone kiosk and the cult of celebrity. It ventured further into nostalgia, reminding him that playing marbles in the street was "the Grand Theft Auto of its day".

Scrumping

We loved scrumping.
Great windfall of youth
It wasn't just the act - but what was heard:
The thumping sound of the word itself
So, let's go scrumping, scrum-ping:
Not stealing, not thieving, just scrumping.
Robbing, as everyone knows, is a crime
But scrumping means rescuing apples in time
Before they rot or decompose
Like a discarded rose
That's beginning to fade.
It had all the thrills of a commando raid
Over the wall and among the trees,
In and out in two minutes. What a breeze.
Beautiful Bramleys and oh richest prize
Cox's Orange Pippin, try them for size.
That was the king of the apple tree
A Garden of Eden moment for me,
A time to savour and feast and sing
Not robbing, not thieving, just scrumping.

Alchemy of Age

Alchemy of Age is Victor Keegan's fourth book of poetry and covers friendship, art, science, London, birth, death and everything in between, as seen through the magic mirror of age. It revels in the magic whereby the alchemy of age can turn base memories into gold.

Shard

Still
Don't
Know
Whether
To like you,
Or hate you.
Too soon yet
To tell I guess.
Like unsought
Liaisons it takes
Time to gel. You
Have invaded my
Personal space, you
Have now shattered
The silence of the sky,
Stalking me wherever I
Walk. Each glimpse I get
Of the city has to include
You; always looking down
On me like a godly chaperone
Even when my back be turned.
Who can tell what future giants
Will follow this precedent you've
Set. Intruders all–I doubt it will ever
Stop now our defences are truly down.

London My London

London My London, Victor's 5th poetry book, covers life from birth amidst the bombs of the Second World War and his belated discovery of London's hidden history. London My London is tribute to the author's heartfelt love of London. It is a compilation of London poems that appeared in earlier books with a raft of new ones.

Necropolis Railway

The Necropolis Railway at Waterloo
Conveyed dead people no matter who
From a station in London's centre, no joking
To a fresh built city for the dead in Woking
No probs as long as you paid for a pass
Which could be first, second, or even third class
As in life, so in death, you must know your place
As well as being in a state of grace.
The most famous customer so history tells
Was Communist founder Frederick Engels
Whose principles should have - oh let it pass
What does it matter if he travelled first class
You don't want dead bodies to lose any face
When you're gone, class distinction leaves no trace.

On arrival at Brookwood, there's a religious test
One station for Protestants and a second for the rest
(Remember - even when you bury your dead,
There's a risk that a religious virus could spread)
So, let's give thanks to the railway of Necropolis
For helping God sort bodies before the Apocalypse.

Selective Memories

Victor Keegan's sixth - and final (maybe)- book of poems reflects his insatiable curiosity about the nature of the universe, how oak trees talk to each other, the pleasures of daydreaming, the shifting archaeology of the Thames foreshore and dozens of other subjects.

Dreams

This life you live, you know what it means,
A shabby journey
Made stable by dreams.

For they are the fuel that stops life stalling.
Forget the present and start recalling.
Don't doubt, dreams are the key
To underlying reality.
Pleasure dreamt
Beats pleasure spent
Reality is the curse
That keeps our dreams apart.
They are the dark energy
That no one else can see,
The invisible force
That keeps our lives on course
As dark energy binds the universe.

All of Victor's books are published by ShakerspearesMonkey and are available to buy online in print and eBook.
viewauthor.at/victorkeegan

Books By Michelle Gordon

WHERE'S MY F**KING UNICORN?

Are your bookshelves filled with self-help books, and yet your life feels empty? Do you keep following paths to enlightenment that lead to the same dead ends? You've read the books, attended the seminars and taken heed of every bit of advice going... but you're still waiting for your f**king unicorn to come along! Where's My F**king Unicorn? is a guide to life, creativity and happiness that offers a very different way forward. Author, Michelle Gordon, explains why, in spite of all your best efforts, your life still doesn't live up to your vision of what it should be, and tells you exactly what you can do about it. In refreshingly down-to-earth language, she shows you how to harness all the self-knowledge you have gained from all those self-help books you've read, and actually start putting it to practical use.

Where's My F**king Unicorn? is published by *Ammonite Press* and is available online and in bookstores.

Earth Angel Series:

THE EARTH ANGEL TRAINING ACADEMY
(book 1)

There are humans on Earth, who are not, in fact, human.

They are **Earth Angels**.

Earth Angels are beings who have come from other realms, dimensions and planets, and are choosing to be born on Earth in human form for just **one** reason.

To **Awaken the world**.

Before they can carry out their perilous mission, they must first learn how to be human.

The best place they can do that, is at

The Earth Angel Training Academy

THE EARTH ANGEL AWAKENING
(book 2)

After learning how to be human at the Earth Angel Training Academy, the Angels, Faeries, Merpeople and Starpeople are born into human bodies on Earth.

Their Mission? **Awaken the world**.

But even though they **chose** to go to Earth, and they chose to be human, it doesn't mean that it will be **easy** for them to Awaken themselves.

Only if they **reconnect** to their **origins**,
and to other Earth Angels, will they will be able to **remember** who they really are.

Only then, will they experience
The Earth Angel Awakening

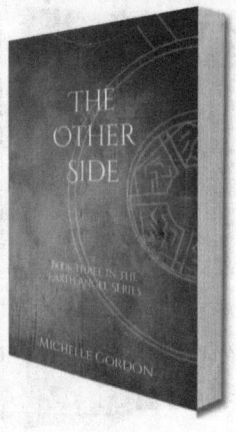 

THE OTHER SIDE
(book 3)

There is an Angel who holds the world in her hands.
She is the **Angel of Destiny**.
Her actions will start the **ripples** that will **save humans** from their certain demise.
In order for her to initiate the necessary changes, she must travel to other **galaxies**, and call upon the most **enlightened** and **evolved** beings of the Universe.
To save **humankind**.
When they agree, she wishes to prepare them for Earth life, and so invites them to attend the Earth Angel Training Academy, on **The Other Side**

THE TWIN FLAME REUNION
(book 4)

The Earth Angels' missions are clear: **Awaken** the world, and move humanity into the **Golden Age**.

But there is another reason many of the Earth Angels choose to come to Earth.

To **reunite** with their **Twin Flames**.

The Twin Flame connection is deep, everlasting and intense, and happens only at the **end of an age**. Many Flames have not been together for millennia, some have never met.

Once on Earth, every Earth Angel longs to meet their Flame. The one who will make them **feel at home**, who will make living on this planet bearable.

But no one knows if they will actually get to experience

The Twin Flame Reunion

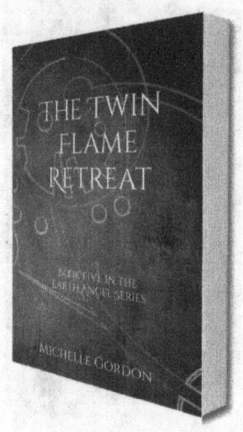

The Twin Flame Retreat
(book 5)

The question in the minds of many Earth Angels
on Earth right now is:

Where is my **Twin Flame?**

Though many Earth Angels are now meeting their Flames, the
circumstances around their reunion can have

life-altering consequences.

If meeting your Flame meant your life would never be the same
again, would you still want to find them?

When in need of **support** and answers,
Earth Angels attend

The Twin Flame Retreat

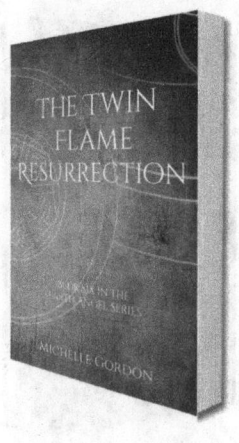

The Twin Flame Resurrection
(book 6)

Twin Flames are **destined** to meet. And when they are meant to be together, nothing can keep them apart.

Not even **death**.

When Earth Angels go home to the Fifth Dimension too soon, they have the **choice** to come back.

To be with their **Twin Flame**.

The connection can be so overwhelming, that some Earth Angels try to resist it, try to push it away.

But it is **undeniable**.

When things don't go according to plan, the universe steps in, and the Earth Angels experience

The Twin Flame Ressurrection

The Twin Flame Reality
(book 7)

Being an Earth Angel on Earth can be difficult, especially when it doesn't feel like home, and when there's a deep longing for a realm or dimension where you feel you **belong**.

Finding a Twin Flame, is like **coming home**.

Losing one, can be **devastating**.

Adrift, lonely, isolated… an Earth Angel would be forgiven for preferring to go home, than to stay here **without their Flame**.

But if they can find the **strength** to stay, to follow their mission to **Awaken** the world, and fulfil their original purpose, they will find they can be **happy** here.

Even despite the sadness of
The Twin Flame Reality

THE TWIN FLAME REBELLION
(book 8)

The Angels on the Other Side have a **duty** to **help** their human charges, but **only** when they are **asked** for help.
They are not allowed to meddle with **Free Will**.
But a number of Angels are asked to break their **Golden Rule**, and start influencing the human lives of the Earth Angels.
Once the Angels start nudging, they find they can't stop, and when the Earth Angels find out they are being manipulated from the Other Side, they aren't happy.
Determined to **choose** their own **fate**,
the Earth Angels embark on
The Twin Flame Rebellion

THE TWIN FLAME REIGNITION
(book 9)

The **destiny** of many **Twin Flames** is changing. Those destined to remain apart on Earth are hearing the call to come **together.**

As things begin to shift and change, it suddenly it seems **possible** for them to **reunite,** and have the lives they always **dreamed** of.

But when **visions** and **dreams** of **Atlantis** begin to plague the Earth Angels, and they try to work out their meaning, what they **discover** may jeopardise **The Twin Flame Reignition**

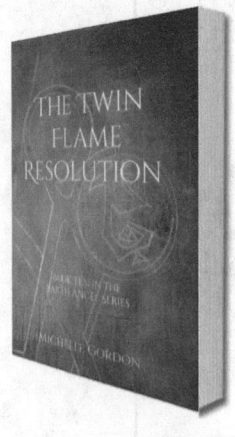 

THE TWIN FLAME RESOLUTION
(book 10)
When a Seer has a **vision** of the **Golden Age**, she takes drastic action in order to make it happen.

The consequences of her actions are so **epic** that the lives of every **Earth Angel** and every **human** on Earth will be altered **forever**.

As well as the unions of all the
Twin Flames.

She enlists the help of two **Angels** to assist her in
The Twin Flame Resolution

Visionary Collection:

Heaven dot com

When Christina goes into hospital for the final time, and knows that she is about to lose her battle with cancer, she asks her boyfriend, James, to help her deliver messages to her family and friends after she has gone.

She also asks him to do something for her, but she dies before he can make it happen, and he finds it difficult to forgive himself.

After her death, her messages are received by her loved ones, and the impact her words have will change their lives forever.

The Doorway to PAM

Natalie is an ordinary girl who has lost her way. There is nothing particularly special about her or her life. She has no exceptional abilities. She hasn't achieved anything miraculous. Her life has very little meaning to it.

Evelyn is the caretaker at Pam's. The alternate dimension where souls at their lowest point find the answers they need to turn their lives around. The dimension dreamers visit, to help people while they sleep.

One ordinary girl, one extraordinary woman.
One fated meeting that will change lives.

The Elphite

Ellie's life is just one long, bad case of déjà vu. She has lived her life before - a hundred times before - and she remembers each and every lifetime.

Each time, she has changed things, but has never managed to change the ending.

This time, in this life, she hopes that it will be different. So she makes the biggest change of all - she tries to avoid meeting him.

Her soulmate. The love of her life.

Because maybe if they don't meet, she can finally change her destiny.

But fate has other ideas...

I'm Here

When Marielle finds out that a guy she had a crush on in school has passed away, the strange occurrences of the previous week begin to make sense. She suspects that he is trying to give her a message from the other side, and so opens up to communicate with him, She has no idea that by doing so, she will be forming a bond so strong, that life as she knows it will forever be changed.

Nathan assumed that when he died, he would move on, and continue his spiritual journey. But instead he finds himself drawn to a girl that he once knew. The more he watches her, and gets to know her, he realises that he was drawn to her for a reason, and that once he knows what that is, he will be able to change his destiny.

The Earth Angel Series and the Visionary Collection are published by *The Amethyst Angel* and are available online in eBook and print.

More Books from Not From this Planet

THE WINTER'S SLEEP
by Monica Cafferky

A fast-paced thriller with a supernatural twist, *The Winter's Sleep* takes the reader on a breathtaking ride from Leeds to the Yorkshire coast in a tale of ghosts, betrayal and fraud.

A handsome husband. A beautiful home. A job she loves.
Yet Brigid Raven is drowning in debts and there's only one way out.
Fake her death and walk away from everything she's struggled so hard to build.
Can she pull off her new identity? How will she survive on the run?
But Brigid has another secret. She can see the dead and now they won't leave her alone.

The Winter's Sleep is published by Jasper Tree Press and is available online in eBook and print.

LITTLE SOMETHING
by Elizabeth Lockwood

Waiting for a little something…A motivational memoir which is as real as it is miraculous. After getting married, trying for a baby was the next logical step. But nothing happened. Nothing. Months and months of nothing. Medical tests showed that there were issues on both sides and treatment would be required to even have a small chance of getting pregnant. But with almost 100 pounds of weight loss standing in the way, Elizabeth Lockwood just couldn't see how it would be possible. But it was, and after losing weight, IVF treatment became a reality. Two treatment cycles later, and no baby, Elizabeth turned to running to aid her mental health. In training for marathons she found a positive way to move forward.But then it all changed… Little Something is about hopes, dreams, and resilience. Finding ways to illuminate the darkness, and never ever giving up. Oh, and the miracles that occur when you least expect them.

Little Something is published by Labradorite Press and is available online in eBook and print.

THE MAGICAL FAERIE DOOR
by Michelle Louise Gordon

*The magical full moon
lights the doorway to Eireaf,
land of the purple sun
and the golden faerie queen*

Lily believes in faeries.

She always has. Even though she had never seen one. Because she believes that there is still magic in the world.

And because the magic inside her is recognised, she is led to the faerie realm, where she is given a very important mission...

The Magical Faerie Door is published by Amber Beetle Books and is available online in eBook and hardback.

Not From This Planet

Not From This Planet is an Independent Publisher on a mission to collaborate with authors to create the best possible books that delight and inspire and entertain – and also pay a fair royalty to the author. They treat every book as it if were their own and they have big have plans to take the publishing world by storm.

NotFromThisPlanet.co.uk

www.ingramcontent.com/pod-product-compliance
Lightning Source LLC
Chambersburg PA
CBHW011317080526
44588CB00020B/2745